Cliveden, Germantown   *1st Overleaf:* Independence Hall   *2nd Overleaf:* Benjamin Franklin Bridge

©Copyright by Foremost Publishers, Inc.

Photographs ©Copyright 1986 in U.S.A. by Robert Llewellyn.

Photographs ©Under UCC 1986 by Robert Llewellyn.

All rights reserved.

This book, or portions thereof, may not be reproduced
in any form without permission of the publisher,
Foremost Publishers, Inc. Photographs may not be reproduced
in any form without permission of Robert Llewellyn.

Edited by James B. Patrick and Lindsay Eckford.

Designed by Donald G. Paulhus.

Printed in Japan.

ISBN 0-89909-097-4

Published by
Foremost Publishers, Inc.
An affiliate of Yankee Publishing Inc.
Dublin, New Hampshire 03444

PHILADELPHIA

Photography by Robert Llewellyn
Introduction by Roger W. Moss

Published by Foremost Publishers, Inc.
An affiliate of Yankee Publishing Inc.

Introduction

In the fall of 1723 an apprentice printer departed Boston to seek his fortune in Philadelphia. Making his way south to the banks of the Delaware at Burlington, New Jersey, he eventually secured passage on a boat headed down river. "About midnight not having yet seen the City," he later wrote, "some of the Company were confident we must have passed it," so they went ashore and spent the night. At first light they discovered themselves to be quite near the city and promptly rowed to the public wharf at the foot of Market Street. In this fashion did the young Benjamin Franklin arrive in the city that would become synonymous with his name.

To this day it is best to arrive in Philadelphia by water, or at least by the wonderfully scenic drives that parallel the banks of the Schuylkill River. These drives twist along the wooded and neatly maintained river banks, putting the occupants of passing automobiles eye-to-eye with blasé Canada Geese or oarlock-level with scullers and local college crews whose flashing blades are nearly a year-round part of the river. Above the flood plain on either side – where the thick foliage dramatically announces seasonal changes – can occasionally be seen the cornice and roof line of a colonial country house or villa and the looming dome of Memorial Hall, a survivor of the Centennial Exposition. The Schuylkill River banks also constitute one of the great sculpture gardens of America and alert the first-time visitor to the approaching city's reputation as a center of public art. Finally the drives sweep into center city and provide, especially on the western approach, the best view of Boathouse Row, the Fairmount Waterworks, the Philadelphia Museum of Art, and, ultimately, the skyline of modern Philadelphia.

Having arrived in the city by the above route or a less scenic one, getting around is not at all difficult. In fact, few American cities are easier. William Penn's Surveyor-General, Thomas Holme, laid out the city in 1682 on a rigid grid system, "so that the streets hereafter may be uniforme downe to the Water from the Country bounds." The resulting rectangle of streets was two miles long and a mile wide, enclosing approximately 1,280 acres between the mighty Delaware River and the less useful but infinitely more picturesque Schuylkill River. Eventually the east-west streets were named for trees – resulting in the jingle,

High, Mulberry, Sassafras, Vine
Chestnut, Walnut, Spruce, and Pine.

For ease of identification the north-south streets were numbered. However, early settlers on the river banks counted back from *both* rivers – requiring each street to be additionally identified as "Schuylkill Second" or "Delaware Third," and so on. (This confusion was eliminated in the nineteenth century; the numbering now begins on the Delaware River side and moves westward to the city's limits.) According to Frances Trollope – mother of the novelist Anthony Trollope – who visited America in the 1820s, the Philadelphia "mode of distinguishing the streets is commodious to strangers, from the facility it gives of finding out where-abouts you are; if you ask for the United States Bank, you are told it is in Chestnut, between Third and Fourth, and as the streets are all divided from each other by equal distances, of about three hundred feet, you are sure of not missing your mark."

The original Philadelphia plan provided that the city should be bisected with a double width north-south street (the Broad Street so beloved of parading New Year's Day Mummers) that would intersect a similarly wide east-west one (High Street, later renamed Market). At the juncture a ten acre square was provided as the heart of the future city. Today Center Square is covered by the exuberant and massive City Hall designed by the High Victorian architect John McArthur, Jr.; when completed in 1901 it was the tallest and largest public building in the United States. As the focus of intense development in modern Philadelphia, Center Square is today closer to being the true heart of the city than at any time in the past three hundred years.

Strategically placed in the seventeenth-century plan were four additional parks, now named for George Washington, David Rittenhouse, Benjamin Franklin, and James Logan. While modern Philadelphians might wish that the original streets had been twelve feet wider, the rational layout and these regularly spaced parks means that in center city Philadelphia one never needs to fear getting lost or being required to walk more than a few "blocks" to reach an oasis of grass, trees, and fountains. Both of these features – as well as impossible rush hour traffic jams – help to make Philadelphia a walker's city. Which is not to suggest that public transportation isn't outstanding. Center city Philadelphia is one of the few major urban areas where it is possible – in fact, highly desirable – not to own an automobile. Here the street dangers are yuppies in Adidas pulling wire shopping carts rather than L.L. Bean-chic suburban preppies with Volvo stationwagons.

According to the statisticians who compile such books as the *Places Rated Almanac*, good public transportation is only one reason Philadelphia ranks among the best metropolitan areas in which to live. There are the museums, libraries, learned societies, musical and dance groups, four-year colleges and universities, medical schools and hospitals, outstanding restaurants, and a salubrious climate – well, we do have four distinct seasons. One suspects that a random, curb-side sampling of Philadelphians might eventually come up with such a list, but there would doubtless be additions ranging from the Flyers, 76ers, and Eagles, to cheesesteak sandwiches, Mummers, funky South Street, proximity to the Jersey Shore, the Liberty Bell, and soft pretzels. In short, the secret of Philadelphia's livability may not be quantifiable, and any attempt to do so suggests the parable of three blind men describing an elephant.

All the world's great cities have certain common features. The first is a mantle of antiquity requiring at least several hundred years to lay down. While an architectural cityscape may have suffered successive intrusions of astounding beauty or unmitigated ugliness, a great city manages to retain its historicity, humane scale, and livability. The neighborhood in which I live is a better than average example. In 1682 Penn granted a charter to a group of Philadelphia merchants who hoped to monopolize the West Indian sugar trade. This Free Society of Traders was also given one hundred acres of real estate between Spruce and Pine Streets where they erected a trading house on a slight rise of land known as the Society's Hill. Over the next one hundred fifty years this area was developed and for much of that time was the most prosperous part of the largest city in America. In the mid-nineteenth century, however, fashionable Philadelphia moved westward to create the wonderfully diverse Rittenhouse Square

neighborhoods. The old city of Colonial and Revolutionary fame and architecture gradually decayed. Following World War II this "most historic square mile in America" became the focus of massive Federal restoration and urban renewal; the great architectural and historic landmarks such as Independence Hall, Carpenters' Hall, the American Philosophical Society, the Second Bank of the United States, and The Athenaeum were restored while private owners and investors renovated hundreds of surrounding eighteenth and nineteenth-century townhouses. Today "Society Hill" ranks with Washington's Georgetown and Boston's Beacon Hill as among the most desirable urban neighborhoods. To balance the loss of housing units created by the introduction of pocket parks and the manicured lawns of Independence National Historical Park, six carefully sited high-rise towers – now condominiums – were introduced. The population base consequently became adequate to support shops, restaurants, and theaters. In the evening our streets are peopled by residents walking home from work, pausing to chat with a neighbor or to kibitz the repainting of a colonial church with schizophrenic Victorian detailing.

Philadelphia has not abandoned its historic core and did not "renew" itself into the frigid isolation imposed on other American cities after World War II. Consequently, the center city neighborhoods have reversed the trend toward declining population that has plagued most urban areas of the northeastern United States.

The Philadelphia celebrated by Robert Llewellyn's photographs is unquestionably a city in transition from beating hammers to the quieter if no less rhymthic pulse of data processing, perhaps appropriate in the city where ENIAC – the first computer – was developed and constructed by J. Presper Eckert and John W. Mauchly. Philadelphia has been "discovered" in the late twentieth century for the same happy location that drew wealth and population two hundred years ago. Sitting astride the Boston-to-Richmond metropolitan corridor, Philadelphia's location offers access to a substantial percentage of the American population with few of the real or perceived disadvantages of its near neighbors. The signs of this awakening interest are most graphically seen in the broad-shouldered, modern skyline west of City Hall that projects above and contrasts starkly with the domestic scale of Philadelphia and has prompted heated debate over just how high these post-industrial smokestacks of progress should be. Most Philadelphians seem to have little trouble with the realities of high-rise office buildings so long as they are located west of City Hall and north of the Rittenhouse Square neighborhoods.

Ironically, the area of the city now under pressure from corporate development also experienced the early twentieth-century City Beautiful Movement that encouraged the replanning of American urban areas to introduce grand vistas, parks, and monumental civic structures. In a successful effort to link Fairmount Park – the largest urban park in the United States – with the center of Philadelphia, a parkway was slashed across Penn's grid to the northwest from Center Square, past Napoleon Le Brun's Cathedral of SS. Peter and Paul, consuming Logan Square, and terminating at the future site of the Philadelphia Museum of Art above the Neo-classical complex of the waterworks on the east bank of the Schuyl-

kill River. To heighten the effect of a new world Champs Elysees, architect Horace Trumbauer designed the Free Library after the Chateau Crillon in Paris. While the resulting Parkway is better suited for military reviews than boulevard strolling, it provides Philadelphia a grand approach to center city and gives Robert Llewellyn enough distance to unlimber his long lens.

Llewellyn has a skillful eye for capturing impressions of a city. This book is not a documentary, yet the Philadelphia that 4 million tourists come to see each year is well represented – the Liberty Bell, Independence Hall, Elfreth's Alley – as are the libraries, museums, and performing arts groups that make Philadelphia a national treasure. But the camera's eye also lets us slip behind the monuments of civic pride to savor the exotic flavors of Chinatown, the hustle and bustle of the Italian market, the effervescence that floods up Broad Street every New Year's Day from the close-knit neighborhoods of South Philadelphia. As you turn the pages that follow, you may begin to understand why those of us fortunate enough to live and work in Philadelphia agree with Sidney George Fisher, who recorded in his diary after an out of town visit in 1839, "Returned to Philad: as I always do, with the conviction that . . . it is the most *comfortable* and desirable place for a residence in this country."

Roger W. Moss,
The Athenaeum of Philadelphia

At the Art Museum

School Children, Liberty Bell

Elfreth's Alley

Arch Street   *Overleaf:* University of Pennsylvania, Looking East

Independence National Historical Park

City Hall

Memorial Hall

Memorial Hall

Overleaf: Assembly Room, Independence Hall

Luthier, Locust Street

Philadelphia Bourse

Athenaeum of Philadelphia *Overleaf:* Skyline, Looking East

Reenactment, Battle of Germantown

Flag of the Revolution, Society Hill

Girard College

Drexel University   *Overleaf:* Joan of Arc by Art Museum

Masonic Temple

St. Peter's Episcopal Church

Japanese House, Fairmont Park

Japanese House, Fairmont Park

Independence Hall   Franklin Institute   *Overleaf:* Benjamin Franklin Parkway, Looking East

Italian Market

Italian Market

City Hall

By City Hall

Overleaf: South Philadelphia

City Council Chamber, City Hall   City Council Caucus Room, City Hall

Pennsylvania Ballet Class

Pennsylvania Ballet Class

North Portal, City Hall

North Portal, City Hall

Overleaf: Boathouse Row

Second Bank of the United States

Fidelity Mutual Building   *Overleaf:* Pennsylvania Academy of Fine Arts

Germantown Avenue

Franklin Court

Pegasus, Memorial Hall

Philadelphia Museum of Art and the Waterworks *Overleaf:* Rittenhouse Square

Merchant's Exchange

Merchant's Exchange

Chinatown

Chinatown *Overleaf:* Schuylkill River

EDW F HOFFMAN III

Skyline, Looking North

Society Hill

Philadelphia Museum of Art

Philadelphia Museum of Art

Overleaf: University of Pennsylvania

Wannamakers by City Hall

John F. Kennedy Boulevard

Church of the Gesu   St. Mark's Church

Mt. Pleasant, Fairmont Park

Boathouse Row

Overleaf: Skyline, Looking West

Temple University

Rittenhouse Square *Overleaf:* City Hall

Free Library

University of Pennsylvania

Overleaf: Penn's Landing

Elfreth's Alley

Doll Shop, Chestnut Hill

Logan Circle

Calder Statue, Logan Circle

Overleaf: Rittenhouse Square

Philadelphia Zoological Gardens

Mansion, *Solitude*, Zoological Gardens

Philadelphia Zoological Gardens

Philadelphia Zoological Gardens *Overleaf: Playing Angels*, Fairmont Park

Olympia, Dewey's Flagship and Society Hill Towers — Cathedral of St. Peter and Paul

Mummers

Mummers

Mummers

Mummers

Overleaf: Benjamin Franklin Bridge

Fountain, Independence Mall

City Hall

Rittenhouse Square

Philadelphia Museum of Art

Liberty Bell